Renate Bethge

# Dietrich Bonhoeffer

A Brief Life

translated by K. C. Hanson

*Fortress Press*
*Minneapolis*

DIETRICH BONHOEFFER
A Brief Life

First English-language edition published by Fortress Press in 2004.

Translated by K. C. Hanson from *Dietrich Bonhoeffer: Eine Skizze seines Leben*, published by Gütersloher Verlaghaus GmbH, Gütersloh, Germany, copyright © 2004.

Photo on p. 74: private archive of the author
All other photos: © Chr. Kaiser/Gütersloher Verlaghaus GmbH, Gütersloh

ISBN 0-8006-3677-5

Cover design: Init GmbH, Bielefeld
Reproduction: scan:light media GmbH, Marienfeld
Printing and binding: GGP Media GmbH, Pössneck
Printed in Germany

08 07 06 05 04   1 2 3 4 5 6 7 8 9 10

# Contents

# Parents

Dietrich Bonhoeffer was the sixth of eight children. He had four sisters and three brothers and, along with his twin sister, he was born on February 4, 1906, in Breslau, Germany. When he was six years old, the family moved to Berlin, where his father, Karl Bonhoeffer, became Professor of Neurology and Psychiatry and the Director of the university neurological clinic. His mother, Paula Bonhoeffer (née von Hase), was a committed Christian, who had grown up as the daughter and granddaughter of theologians. She was lively, cheerful, and full of dreams. She could overlook the minor mistakes of her children, but she would not tolerate inconsiderateness and unkindness to others.

Paula Bonhoeffer passed the "teacher's examination for higher education," which was quite unusual at the time. Few girls went on for higher education, and she had many discussions with her parents about her plans. Bonhoeffer's mother even taught her own children in the first years, along with a couple friends of the same age. But once she had eight children, it became too much to handle, and she had to take on another teacher to help her. She reserved the religion class for herself, however.

*Dietrich's parents: Karl and Paula Bonhoeffer as a young married couple in Breslau (around 1900)*

Bonhoeffer's father was reserved in appearance
and very critical of any type of arrogance. Simplicity
and clarity were his supreme commandments.
Dietrich Bonhoeffer often emphasized in later years
what positive effects these characteristics of his
parents had on his upbringing and lifestyle.

*Dear Mama,*

*I want you and Papa to know that you are constantly in*
*my thoughts, and that I thank God for all you have been*
*to me and the rest of the family. I know you have always*
*lived for us, and have never had a life of your own.*
*And that is why there is no one else with whom I can*
*share all that I am going through.*

Dietrich Bonhoeffer from prison to his parents (December 28, 1944)

# Childhood and Youth

The Bonhoeffer children had a harmonious and fulfilling childhood. To be sure, their parents demanded respect from their children, but at the same time gave them a great deal of freedom. They tried to encourage each child in his or her individual interests and abilities. Among other things, all the children had music lessons – Dietrich Bonhoeffer played the piano remarkably well. There was no shortage of books and games. Their mother gave wonderful children's parties, and governesses took care of the children. Furthermore, numerous visitors to the Bonhoeffers' home offered many interesting encounters and stimuli for them.

*In gratitude, I achieve the right relation to my past. In it, the past becomes useful for the present.*

The seven oldest Bonhoeffer children, L to R:
Sabine, Dietrich, Christine, Ursula, Klaus, Walter, and Karl-Friedrich

At seventeen (1923), Dietrich Bonhoeffer passed his graduation examination (*Arbitur*) and began his theological studies in Tübingen, where he occasionally lived with his grandmother.

*Dietrich Bonhoeffer as a student (about 1923)*

In the summer of 1924, Dietrich traveled to Rome with his brother Klaus. Both brothers were already familiar with this city and its history from reading, school, and discussions at home, and they were full of anticipation. They were not disappointed.

*In Rome (May 1924)*

Dietrich wrote in his journal about what he did on this trip:

> *When I saw the Laocoon for the first time, I actually shuddered; it is incredible.*

*Laocoon group*

Yet in Tegel Prison twenty years later, Bonhoeffer reflected in a letter, written on January 23, 1944, to Eberhard Bethge, who was serving in the area of Rome as a soldier:

> *If you see the Laocoon [statue] again, see if you don't think that it (the father's head) is not possibly the model for later images of Christ.*

In Rome, Dietrich's encounter with the Catholic church – which played only a minor role in Berlin at that time – was very important. In his journal he noted:

> *Palm Sunday. . . the first day that something of the reality of Catholicism dawned on me, nothing romantic or the like, but rather that I am beginning, I believe, to understand the concept "church."*

It was not easy for him to leave Rome. His journal notes:

> When I looked at St. Peter's for the last time, there
> was a pain around my heart, and I quickly got on
> the trolleycar and left . . .

*St. Peter's Plaza in Rome (around 1920)*

After the trip to Italy, Dietrich Bonhoeffer returned home and set to work in earnest on his studies in Berlin. Not only was he busy, however, with his tasks at the university; he also participated completely in what Berlin had to offer: concerts, theaters, and museums. Besides that, he had an active life at home with his many siblings and friends. They went on trips, arranged parties, and also often went to dances. His mother always had good ideas for these occasions, and even years later one heard from the participants how much they enjoyed these festivities.

*Rome, St. Paul's Outside the Wall (San Paolo fuori le mura); a postcard that Bonhoeffer saved from Rome of the church that especially impressed him.*

*Dietrich proposed to celebrate the first beautiful days of
spring in April with a journey through the countryside.
Through it all, we were a very happy group. We stopped
wherever we pleased, and in the afternoon we planned our
itinerary to the next village. We sent two ahead to arrange
accommodations – in any inn, never in youth hostels.*

*Susanne Dress (née Bonhoeffer)*

*Journey through the countryside in April 1927; L to R: Walter Dress (later the husband of Susanne Bonho-
effer), Ilse Dress, Dietrich and Susanne Bonhoeffer, Grete von Dohnanyi (later the wife of Karl-Friedrich
Bonhoeffer).*

In the winter of 1927/28, Dietrich passed his first
theological examination and submitted his doctoral
dissertation, *Sanctorum Communio*, which was
published in 1930.

# Vicar in Barcelona

After completing his studies, Dietrich became a
vicar to the German congregation in Barcelona
for a year. This may have presented a somewhat
difficult situation for the pastor who was there,
since the tranquility of the community was
suddenly upset. Bonhoeffer encouraged new
ways of doing things and reinvigorated the old.
Whenever he led the worship service or the
children's worship, the church was full.
Naturally, the country itself also fascinated the
young vicar. He visited Cordoba, Seville, Granada,
and Madrid. With the encouragement of his
brother Klaus, who already knew Spain, he came
to enjoy the bullfights.

Dietrich sent his brother-in-law, Rüdiger Schleicher, a postcard "with greetings from the matador," with a witty photo-montage of him as a great bullfighter on it.

Dietrich was completely engaged in the community, becoming a member of the "German clubs": the German tennis and glee clubs. His talents in music, chess, and athletics were, at the same time, beneficial.

*Dietrich Bonhoeffer with children at the children's worship service in Barcelona (1928)*

Nevertheless he retained his critical perspective. He wrote about the community in a rather detached way:

> *These people relate to the church probably just as positively as they do to sports or the German National Party, only less actively.*

And Bonhoeffer's stance toward his theology changed through his interactions with members of the community. At the end of his time in Spain he wrote in his Spain-journal:

> *My theology is beginning to become humanistic; what does this mean? Was Barth ever abroad?*

His supervisor, Pastor Olbricht, sent Bonhoeffer off
with fulsome praise and wrote the following letter on
January 1, 1929:

> *To the German Protestant Church Committee of Berlin,*
> *I faithfully communicate concerning my vicar Lic. theol.*
> *Bonhoeffer, who completes his year and returns home on*
> *February 15. He proved in every way to be very efficient*
> *and helped me greatly in my various activities. He was*
> *especially able to attract the children, whom he loves more*
> *than anything, to the services. His worship services for*
> *children were attended on average by forty children.*
> *He has enjoyed the greatest popularity in the whole*
> *[expatriate] community. I would be ever so grateful if the*
> *German Protestant Church Committee could send me a*
> *new, efficient vicar as soon as possible, who would be just*
> *as active.*
> *With great respect, F. Olbricht, pastor*

# Berlin - New York - Berlin

Back again in Berlin, Bonhoeffer dedicated
himself to his studies, taking his second theological
examination in 1930 for his "habilitation," the final
step in his graduate work. Because he was still too
young to take on an independent pastorate, he
enrolled for a year of study at Union Theological
Seminary in New York. Here he developed close
friendships and had important experiences in both
theological and church work – not least through his
involvement with the Abyssinian Baptist Church in
Harlem and the Social Gospel movement. To imagine
that Bonhoeffer's stay in America was purely academic
would be mistaken. Here he questioned and tested his
ways of thinking and his emotions.

For more than six months I have been at one of the
large Negro Baptist churches in Harlem almost every
Sunday from noon to 2:30. I have heard the gospel
preached in the Negro churches.

Storefront church in Harlem

Bonhoeffer regularly received mail from his home in Berlin. In November 1930, his brother Klaus wrote:

> Since you left, the political situation has changed a lot. The success of National Socialism has convinced the widest circles that the democratic regime has failed during the past ten years. Domestic reasons are used to explain the consequences of the international economic crisis. People are flirting with fascism. I am afraid if this radical wave seizes the intelligentsia, all is up with the poets and thinkers.

Bonhoeffer returned to Germany in 1930 – to a country on the brink of political upheaval. In addition to his work as an instructor (*Privatdozent*) at the university, he became the chaplain for students at the technical school. During this period, he also began his ecumenical work. He was selected to be the youth secretary for the World Alliance for Promoting International Friendship through the Churches.

But mostly Bonhoeffer busied himself during this period with a confirmation group in the Prenzlauer Berg neighborhood. The pastor had not been successful with this confirmation group. So at the beginning, Bonhoeffer let the confirmands run wild; then he stood silently at the wall in front of them and began to speak very softly about the black children in Harlem. The confirmands could not help but listen and soon were fascinated. Gradually, Bonhoeffer developed closer contact with the children living in oppressive situations. He was concerned about them in a personal way, spending weekends with them, bringing them to his family's vacation house in Friedrichsbrunn in the Harz region, and, with the help of his mother, provided each child with a confirmation suit.

*Bonhoeffer with the Berlin confirmands in Friedrichsbrunn (Easter 1932)*

# The Beginning of the Nazi Era

In 1933, the year Adolf Hitler seized power, there
were decisive changes in Bonhoeffer's life. He firmly
supported the church's opposition to the new regime.
In the period immediately following January 31,
1933, Bonhoeffer spoke on a radio broadcast that
was cut off, in which he commented that a leader
who would make himself the idol of his followers
would become a misleader.

During his lecture "The Church and the Jewish
Question" three months later, some of the audience
left the hall irritated. Bonhoeffer had pointed out
the obligation of the church "to question the state
repeatedly whether its actions could be justified, i.e.,
as actions in which law and order are created, not
lawlessness and disorder."

He had also spoken about the possibility that the church, "not just bandage the victims under the wheel, but rather break the spokes of the wheel itself." Already the thought of political resistance rings out here, even if Bonhoeffer was still trying to act solely through his actions within the church. At the same time, he attempted to obtain support from foreign countries through his ecumenical work.

*Boycott of Jewish businesses (1933)*

# London

In October 1933, Bonhoeffer accepted a pastoral appointment to a German congregation in London. The decision to take this on was not easy, as he wrote eight days after his appointment in a detailed letter to Karl Barth – someone who is still famous and Bonhoeffer's well-regarded professor of theology:

*If one were going to discover quite definite reasons for such decisions after the event, one of the strongest, I believe, was that I simply did not any longer feel up to the questions and demands that came to me. I feel that, in some way I don't understand, I find myself in radical opposition to all my friends; I became increasingly isolated with my views of things, even though I was and remain personally close to these people. All this has frightened me and shaken my confidence so that I began to fear that.*

*dogmatism might be leading me astray—since there seemed*

*no particular reason why my own view in these matters*

*should be any better, any more right, than the views of*

*many really capable pastors whom I sincerely respect …*

Karl Barth answered Bonhoeffer on November 20, 1933, with a long, urgent, and yet humorous letter:

*Dear Colleague!*

*You can deduce from the very way in which I address*

*you that I do not regard your departure for England as*

*anything but a necessary personal interlude. Once you*

*had this thing on your mind, you were quite right not to*

*ask for my wise counsel first. I would have advised you*

*against it absolutely, and probably by bringing up my*

*heaviest artillery. And now, as you are mentioning the*

*matter to me after the fact, I can honestly not tell you*

*anything but "Hurry back to your post in Berlin!" …*

*Karl Barth (around 1930)*

With your splendid theological armor and your upright
German figure, should you not perhaps be almost a little
ashamed at a man like Heinrich Vogel, who, wizened and
worked up as he is, is just always there, waving his arms
like a windmill and shouting "Confession! Confession!" in
his own way – in power or in weakness, that doesn't matter
so much – actually giving his testimony? … Be glad that I
do not have you here in person, for I would let go at you
urgently in quite a different way, with the demand that you
must now let go of all these intellectual flourishes and special
considerations, however interesting they may be, and think
of only one thing – that you are a German, that the house of
your church is on fire, that you know enough and can say
what you know well enough to be able to help, and that you
must return to your post by the next ship. Given the situation,
shall we say the ship after next? …

Please take it [this letter] in the friendly spirit in which
it is intended. If I were not so attached to you, I would not
let fly at you in this way.

With sincere greetings,

   Karl Barth

In London, Bonhoeffer now naturally sought contact with the ecumenical movement. He found a sympathetic ear for the political problems of the church in Germany with George Bell, the Bishop of Chichester. Bell, a confirmed pacifist, allowed Bonhoeffer to inform him regularly about the situation of the German church. And Bell's interest was very important to Bonhoeffer because he hoped and fought for Bell's support of the anti-Nazi movement within the German church. So he wrote on March 14, 1934, in preparation for the famous Barmen Synod, which – unlike the initial plan and as mentioned in the letter – first took place at the end of May 1934:

> My Lord Bishop,
>
> May I just let you know that I was called last week again to Berlin—this time by the church authorities. The subject was the ecumenical situation. I also saw [Martin] Niemöller, [Gerhard] Jacobi, and some friends from the Rhineland. The Free Synod in Berlin has made real progress and success. We hope to get ready for a Free National Synod on April 18 in Barmen.

*One of the most important things is that the Christian
churches of the other countries do not lose their interest in
the conflict due to the passage of time. I know that my
friends are looking to you and your further actions with
great hope. There is really a moment now as perhaps never
before in Germany in which our faith in the ecumenical
task of the churches can be shaken and destroyed
completely or strengthened and renewed in a surprisingly
new way. And it is you, my Lord Bishop, on whom it
depends whether this moment shall be seized. The question
at stake in the German church is no longer an internal
issue but is the question of the existence of Christianity
in Europe ...*

George K. A. Bell (1883-1958),
Lord Bishop of Chichester

And on April 7, 1934, he pressed the Swiss theologian
H. L. Henriod, who, like Bonhoeffer himself, belonged
to the secretariat of the ecumenical youth commission,
with the same intention:

> *My dear Henriod!*
>
> *I would very much have liked to discuss the situation with
> you again, since the slowness of ecumenical procedure is
> beginning to look to me like irresponsibility. A decision
> must be made at some point, and it's no good waiting
> indefinitely for a sign from heaven that will solve the
> difficulty without further trouble. Even the ecumenical
> movement has to make up its mind and is therefore subject
> to error, like everything human. But to procrastinate and
> prevaricate simply because you're afraid of erring, when
> others – I mean our brethren in Germany – must make
> infinitely more difficult decisions every day, seems to me
> almost to run counter to love. To delay or fail to make
> decisions may be more sinful than to make wrong decisions.*

out of faith and love. "Allow me to go before . . . ," says the Gospel – how often we use this as an excuse! – and in this particular case, it really is now or never. "Too late" means "never." Should the ecumenical movement fail to realize this, and if there are none who are violent in order to take the kingdom of heaven by force (Matthew 11:12), then the ecumenical movement is no longer the church, but a useless association in which fine speeches are made. "If you do not believe, you will not be established"; to believe, however, means to decide. And can there be any doubt as to the nature of that decision? For Germany today it is the Confession, as it is the Confession for the ecumenical movement. We must shake off our fear of this word – the cause of Christ is at stake, and are we to be found sleeping?

In addition to taking care of his congregation
and participating in the ecumenical movement,
Bonhoeffer especially had the fugitives from
Germany on his heart – both Jews and those
banished by the Nazis for political reasons. He
also asked Bell to help these people. Bell was very
much on for this, as were several members of
Bonhoeffer's congregation.

In August 1934, still in Bonhoeffer's London period,
a major ecumenical conference took place in Fanö,
Denmark. Before he promised to give his address
there, he fought hard for only members of the
Confessing Church to be invited from Germany.
In the German Confessing Church, pastors and
congregations had united in the previously
mentioned Barmen Synod (on May 30, 1934), which
spoke out against the national church (*Reichskirche*),
controlled and unified by the National Socialists.
Bonhoeffer reached a compromise in Fanö.

Only representatives of the national church were allowed; Dietrich Bonhoeffer, however, took part in the conference along with many of his former students from the University of Berlin. His peace speech in Fanö was commented upon at the time and is noted even into our own era and repeatedly quoted:

> *There is no way to peace along the way of safety.*
> *For peace must be dared, it is itself the great venture,*
> *and can never be safe. Peace is the opposite of security.*
> *To demand guarantees is to mistrust, and this mistrust*
> *in turn brings forth war. To look for guarantees is to*
> *want to protect oneself. Peace means giving oneself*
> *completely to God's commandment, wanting no security,*

*but in faith and obedience laying the destiny of the nations in the hand of Almighty God, not trying to direct it for selfish purposes. Battles are won, not with weapons, but with God. They are won when the way leads to the cross.*

*Fanö, Denmark (August 1934); L to R:*
*Inge Karding, Lotte Kühn, Otto Dudzus, Dietrich Bonhoeffer, an unidentified Swede*

# The Preacher's Seminary at Finkenwalde

In April 1935, the Confessing Church asked Dietrich Bonhoeffer to return to Germany, to take on and lead its illegally established preacher's seminary. This was an educational venue for theologians who were preparing for the pastorate after their study at the university. Bonhoeffer postponed his burning desire to learn something about nonviolent resistance in India – he had already made an appointment with Mahatma Gandhi – and followed the call to Pomerania. For some time, he had planned to go to India. His grandmother from Tübingen had already gone to India in 1928 to look around herself. And Dietrich had also hoped to be able to learn something there for the German situation.

But now he was to lead a preacher's seminary.

In doing this, he had himself evaded the obligation

to attend such a seminary.

The vicars who came to the preacher's seminary at

Finkenwalde had already decided for the Confessing

Church and against the national church.

*Fourth Course at Finkenwalde (taken March 14, 1937);*
*O = Dietrich Bonhoeffer; X = Eberhard Bethge*

The time in Finkenwalde marked the young
theologians for the rest of their lives. Along with
them, Bonhoeffer led a consistent Christian life;
and in partnership with him, the young theologians
gained the power to withstand the burdens and
oppressions that they were exposed to in their work
within the Confessing Church. Bonhoeffer collected
his lectures on common life in his book *Life Together*.
Next to *Letters and Papers from Prison*, it has had
the widest distribution to date. It was immediately
reprinted three times the year it appeared. Quite
simple, obvious, but also often forgotten rules of
living together are found here:

*Nobody is too good for the lowest service. Those who*
*worry about the loss of time entailed by such small,*
*outward acts of helpfulness are usually taking their*
*own work too seriously. We must be ready to allow*
*ourselves to be interrupted by God, who will thwart our*

*plans and frustrate our ways time and again, even daily,*
*by sending people across our path with their demands and*
*requests. We can, then, pass them by, preoccupied with*
*our more important daily tasks, just as the priest – perhaps*
*reading the Bible – passed by the man who had fallen*
*among robbers.*

In the Finkenwalde preacher's seminary, they
engaged in serious theology and carefully observed
and discussed politics and church politics. The
pressures from within and without to subject
themselves to the national church were strongly felt
by many of the vicars. Above all, after seminary
was over, they stood alone functioning in their
congregations, needing support.

*Bonhoeffer with seminarians at the Baltic Sea (summer 1936)*

Bonhoeffer regularly sent out a newsletter. In the
newsletter for Christmas 1937, he wrote:

> *This time the annual balance sheet pretty well speaks for*
> *itself. Twenty-seven of your circle have been in prison,*
> *in many cases for several months. Some are there still and*
> *have spent the entire Advent in prison. Of the others, there*
> *cannot be anyone who has not had some sort of experience*
> *either in his work or in his private life of the increasingly*
> *impatient attacks by the anti-Christian forces.*

In 1937 the police shut down the seminary; he continued the work, however, underground. In 1940 then, the final prohibition came. In the meantime, many of the vicars were taken into the armed forces; many of them died between 1939 and 1945.

Most of the survivors were influenced by their time in Finkenwalde throughout their lives. And for Bonhoeffer as well, this time was very significant. He wrote already at the end of 1935 that this had been "the fullest time of my life, both professionally and personally." He was able to work with like-minded and only slightly younger men, who appreciated him and listened to his opinions and advice; and in doing this, he also had a broader impact, even though he was un-popular with the political authorities.

# Friends

Especially meaningful during this period was the
quickly developing friendship with Eberhard Bethge,
who attended the first Finkenwalde course as a
ministerial candidate. Bonhoeffer quickly pulled
Bethge into the responsibility of assisting him until
the closing of the preacher's seminary, and he
remained after that as well in permanently close
contact with Bonhoeffer. In Bonhoeffer's room in
his parent's home in Marienburger Allee, there was
also a bed for Bethge, who often stayed there with him.

Next door, at the house of Bonhoeffer's sister Ursula and his brother-in-law Rüdiger Schleicher, Dietrich and Eberhard often played music together. Dietrich accompanied Eberhard's singing, usually art songs by Wolf, or they played "Art of the Fugue" (Bach) on the piano and spinet. More than anything, however, they practiced cantatas in the larger Bonhoeffer family under Bethge's direction, accompanied by the stringed instruments of the Schleicher family.

*Bonhoeffer's parents' house, adjoining the house of their daughter and son-in-law, Ursula and Rüdiger Schleicher, Marienburger Allee 42 and 43 (October 1, 1935)*

Later in prison, Dietrich was reminded of this and
wrote to Eberhard in a letter on March 1, 1944:

> *The intellectual development of the youngsters was*
> *undoubtedly determined decisively by the type of playing*
> *you introduced and energetically led, that became for*
> *them (much stronger than, for example, for me as a boy)*
> *an element of general human development … I am*
> *convinced that for the Dohnanyi and Schleicher children*
> *the memory of all this will remain forever linked with the*
> *memory of the time of their first intellectual development.*

*Dietrich Bonhoeffer with Eberhard Bethge*

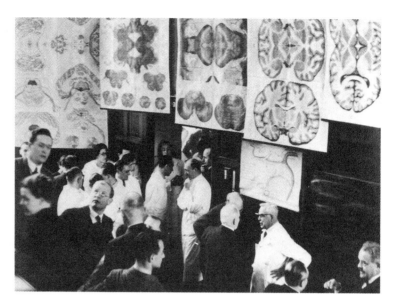

*Farewell lecture of Bonhoeffer's father (1938); on the left, Eberhard Bethge, Dietrich and Karl-Friedrich Bonhoeffer; on the right, Karl Bonhoeffer in conversation with his colleagues Stöckel and Sauerbruch; far right, von Eicken.*

Bonhoeffer also saw to it that Bethge participated in whatever happened in his family. So, for example, both of them attended Karl Bonhoeffer's farewell lecture in July 1938. And Bethge was quite obviously also involved in the large birthday parties for Bonhoeffer's parents and in the "artistic" preparations for them.

Later Bonhoeffer wrote to Bethge from prison:

> *It is probably no accident that you, so to speak, grew entirely into our family, that you were counted as part of it, before you actually belonged to it …*

Shortly before Dietrich Bonhoeffer's arrest, Bethge secretly married Bonhoeffer's niece, Renate, in a civil ceremony, and so his young fiancée spared him from entering military service, which everyone who had graduated had to perform.

Dietrich Bonhoeffer served as witness at this wedding, which had to remain as low-profile as possible given how very young the bride was. Obviously they had planned that Dietrich would marry the couple in a church wedding; but this was not possible because of Bonhoeffer's subsequent arrest.

After Bonhoeffer's death, Bethge dedicated himself completely to the deciphering and editing of Bonhoeffer's writings. His letters from prison – Bethge himself was primarily the one who corresponded with him – quickly made Bonhoeffer well known outside of the church and outside of Germany.

Before Eberhard Bethge, Bonhoeffer had another close friend – Franz Hildebrandt. Dietrich had intense theological discussions with him, always with great wit.

At the beginning of the Nazi era, Bonhoeffer and Hildebrandt planned actions and strategies against the "German Christians" (*Deutsche Christen* or *DC*) together, an originally rather large group of churches influenced strongly by the Nazi administration (*NS-DAP*). The DC wanted to do away with the Old Testament and introduce the "Aryan Clauses," which meant a ban on work for Jews. The ban was also instituted in the church as well, which deterred some of the initial DC-followers, so that this group became somewhat smaller. Franz Hildebrandt was a so-called "half-Jew." His Jewish mother, with whom he lived, also lived in Berlin-Grunewald. After he was imprisoned for his activities in Martin Niemöller's church in Dahlem, he was able to emigrate to England together with his mother, helped by the Bonhoeffer family.

*Franz Hildebrandt*

# Contacts with Jews

The Bonhoeffer family, and especially Dietrich and his siblings, had close contact with Jews, since in Berlin at that time liberal Jews were completely integrated into social life. Nicolaus Sombart writes that in the Grunewald neighborhood, in which the Bonhoeffers lived from 1912 to 1935, every third house belonged to a Jewish family. All of the Bonhoeffer children had close Jewish friends, their father had Jewish assistants, and above all Dietrich's twin sister, Sabine, married a man of Jewish origin, the constitutional lawyer Gerhard Leibholz. To be sure, he had been raised a Christian; but that did not interest the Nazis whatsoever. So for the Bonhoeffers, the provisions and laws against the Jews were an immediate and concrete threat to people close to them, and they recognized the danger more clearly than many Jews themselves.

*The Bonhoeffer family residence in the Grunewald neighborhood of Berlin, Wangenheimstrasse 14*

In September 1938, before the so-called "Crystal Night" (*Kristallnacht*), the Leibholzs fled to England with both their daughters. Dietrich's friend, Bishop Bell of Chichester, was a great help with this. For his part, Bell was informed now through Leibholz about the conditions and background in Germany.

From 1938 on, Bell was a member of the House of Lords. He repeatedly used this new forum effectively. So he corresponded – often more than once a week – with the lawyer from Germany, whom he recommended to friends as "a scholar of European reputation and a man of highest capacity" (November 21, 1941).

*SS and police lead arrested Jews from Berlin to the gathering places for transport to concentration camps after the "Night of the State Pogrom" in November 1938*

Bell used Leibholz's knowledge and abilities in
order to draw the right conclusions from the meager
stream of secret or half-official sources concerning
the situation in Germany. And Leibholz was involved
more actively than ever and took great interest in the
political resistance of his friends at home.

He made attempts that were increasingly desperate,
to lend them support in the English context – all the
more so since he saw the noose around many of his
threatened relatives in Berlin up close.

*Gerhard Leibholz*

# The Second Trip to America

Dietrich Bonhoeffer worked primarily with his vicars in the so-called "collective pastorate," which moved to Sigurdshof (Pomerania) in April 1939.

But always more threatening was the danger that Bonhoeffer would be summoned for military service. When the draft notice finally arrived, his father obtained another deferment for him since Dietrich had an invitation to lecture in America. Dietrich had come to know many people and made many friends during his first stay in America who were now worried about him. So he traveled to London in June, where he visited his sister and brother-in-law, and then went on to New York. Everyone knew that the war was imminent and that Bonhoeffer's situation would become increasingly more difficult. Escaping to America seemed a good solution to his increasing danger.

Yet the thought of leaving family and friends in their difficulties, and even sitting on the sidelines in safety, became increasingly intolerable for Bonhoeffer. So after six weeks he returned to Germany, even though his American friends tried to get him to stay.

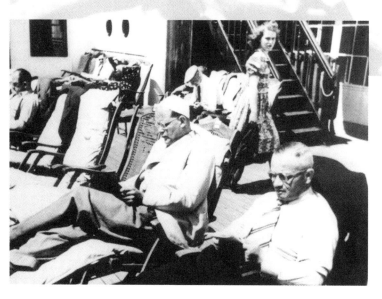

*Dietrich Bonhoeffer onboard the* Bremen *on his trip to the U.S.*

Previously he had written to Prof. Reinhold Niebuhr:

> *I have come to the conclusion that I made a mistake*
> *in coming to America. I have to live through the difficult*
> *period of our national history with the Christians in*
> *Germany. I will have no right to assist with the*
> *restoration of Christian life after the war in Germany if*
> *I do not share the tests of this period with my people.*

Bonhoeffer knew that his return would be dangerous.
Because of continual reprisals, the Confessing Church
had become weaker and was no longer capable of
effective public actions. For this reason Bonhoeffer
concluded that he had to engage himself politically.
His political resistance derived solely from his church
resistance.

# Conspiratorial Trips

Hans von Dohnanyi, the husband of Bonhoeffer's
second oldest sister, Christine, worked for Admiral
Wilhelm Canaris in the Office for Counterespionage.
Both belonged to an opposition group that strove
to assist oppressed Jews and document the crimes of
the National Socialists, and they later worked to
assassinate Hitler.

*Dr. Hans von Dohnanyi*

*Admiral Canaris*

In this group, many threads of the resistance converged. About 1940, Bonhoeffer became a so-called V-man (for special duty), and through this he escaped the danger of being drafted into military service. Officially, he was supposed to make available his foreign contacts for counterespionage; but in reality he was placed there for resistance.

Bonhoeffer traveled for the Intelligence Service (*Abwehr*) to Switzerland, Norway, Sweden, and Italy (Rome). He was commissioned to find out how the Americans and English would react in the event of a coup. Would their plans for war change? Once again he met his English friend, Bishop Bell, on this mission in Stockholm, and Bell was attempting to do everything he could in London to support German resistance. Bell did not find a sympathetic hearing, however, and was given no credence within his government. A positive answer would have greatly encouraged the German generals in their decision to go ahead with the coup. On his trip to Switzerland, Dietrich had hoped to be able to visit Karl Barth. But this suddenly appeared to be awkward.

Dietrich had heard in Switzerland that Karl Barth thought it was "somewhat uncanny" that Bonhoeffer had a passport and could repeatedly travel abroad at a time when only members of the National Socialist government and its representatives were allowed to travel.

*War Department, Berlin, Tirpitz-Ufer; location of the Office of Foreign Espionage (Abwehr).*

So he wrote to Barth on May 17, 1942:

*Dear Professor!*

*Please excuse me if what I now write is nonsense and not worth saying. But I have to ask you because the matter concerns me very much: when I heard last week in Zurich for the first time that "you mistrusted my stay here because of my mission," I just laughed. ... Now I've heard the same thing a second time here in Geneva, and after having thought about it for a couple of days, I just want to tell you that . . . at a time when so much must be based simply on personal trust, everything is finished when mistrust emerges.*

*Karl Barth, 1942*

The answer was very positive, so Dietrich then actually did visit Barth.

# Ethics

In addition to all his political and church tasks and
activities in the resistance against the National
Socialist regime, Bonhoeffer's theological work
remained important to him. He began his *Ethics*,
in which he grappled with questions concerning
responsibility in both political and private arenas.
He was unable, however, to complete the book. After
the war, Eberhard Bethge published the work as he
believed Bonhoeffer would have put it together, at
the request of Bonhoeffer's parents.

Bonhoeffer wrote on ethics mostly at home in
Berlin, even though in 1938 he had been banned
from staying in the city. His father, however, had
obtained permission for him to be allowed to visit
his parents in Berlin, where he was the only one of
his unmarried siblings who still had a room in his
parents' home.

Because of the proximity of the Schleichers and
their four children, he always had an active life in
both houses. Klaus Bonhoeffer and his family also
lived in the vicinity and often came to visit, as did
the von Dohnanyi family. The family life in both
houses – playing music together, conversations,
the intensive exchange of ideas, especially about
political events and developments – all of this
was important for everyone in this difficult
and anxious time.

*Benedictine monastery in Ettal.*

In order to write, Bonhoeffer also spent long
periods in the Bavarian monastery at Ettal and
time and again had some quieter days in Pomerania
due to the kindness of Mrs. Ruth von Kleist-Retzow.
Mrs. Kleist-Retzow was very interested in theology
and had also helped Bonhoeffer in Finkenwalde
with numerous things when the preacher's seminary
had to be constructed out of nothing.

She had come to his worship services there, along with her grandchildren. Bonhoeffer had also confirmed some of her grandchildren, though certainly not the twelve-year-old Maria von Wedemeyer, whom he also met at this time. Dietrich and Maria then met again years later when her grandmother lay in a Berlin hospital and Maria came to see her. Bonhoeffer also visited Mrs. von Kleist-Retzow.

*With Ruth and Konstantin von Kleist-Retzow in Kieckow (1942)*

During this period, Dietrich and Maria grew closer, so that in November 1942 Dietrich spoke with Maria's mother, Ruth von Wedemeyer, about his intention to marry Maria. Maria's mother, however, was of the opinion that her nineteen-year-old daughter was too young to get married and insisted on a year of separation so that Maria could take a break. Naturally, neither of them was happy about this.

*Maria von Wedemeyer (taken in 1942)*

Maria called Dietrich in January 1943 and told him that she wanted to abide by her mother's insistence on waiting a year, but that she was determined to marry him then. From that time on, they regarded themselves as engaged, even though no one other than Eberhard Bethge knew about it.

# Prison

Bonhoeffer's conspiratorial work was finally discovered. On April 5, 1943, the Gestapo arrested him, along with Hans von Dohnanyi and his wife. Christine von Dohnanyi was released from prison after five weeks.

Although Bonhoeffer had always reckoned on being arrested, his time in prison was at first very difficult. He was isolated in a dirty cell, and no one spoke a word to him. Every ten days he was allowed to receive letters from his parents, and he was allowed to answer them as well. Each week he was permitted a package of clean clothes, which could also contain food and books. While his engagement to Maria von Wedemeyer was not yet public, his imprisonment lasted so long that eventually he was allowed to write her and receive her letters.

Dohnanyi and Bonhoeffer
were incarcerated in different
prisons. After a while,
Bonhoeffer found friendly
guards in Tegel Prison who
tried to make life more
tolerable for him. The
commander of the prison even
called his parents after heavy
air attacks in order to tell them
that nothing had happened
to their son. In this way
Bonhoeffer also often received
messages from his parents
after air raids.

*Dietrich Bonhoeffer in the yard of the military interrogation
prison at Tegel (summer 1944)*

Other than his fiancée and his parents, Dietrich
was not allowed to write anyone. He was, however,
allowed to receive letters. For some, it did not seem
advisable to communicate through letters that might
draw the attention of the Gestapo, which controlled
the postal service. Two guards were stationed there
especially for Bonhoeffer. They smuggled letters out
of prison to Bethge and let answers go through to
particular addresses. If this had been discovered,
they could have expected severe punishment.
When Bethge was himself arrested at the end of
October 1944, he destroyed the last letters arranged
for by Bonhoeffer in order to bring neither of them
into even greater danger. He – and many Bonhoeffer-
followers – later regretted that very much, since from
the correspondence with his parents, but above all
with Eberhard Bethge, and from notes that
Bonhoeffer had made in prison, after the war the

book *Letters and Papers from Prison* (*Widerstand und Ergebung*) appeared, which Eberhard Bethge published (at the request of Fritz Bissinger of Chr. Kaiser Publishing House and in consultation with the Bonhoeffer families).

Originally, to be sure, everything personal – as far as it was unnecessary for understanding the letters – was left out of the book. It has often not been understood that the "*Letters to a Friend*" were addressed to Bethge himself. Even today this is frequently not recognized, although it is clarified in the later editions.

In addition to his reputation among German theologians and in church circles, with *Letters and Papers from Prison* Bonhoeffer's name became renowned throughout the world. It is read in Europe, North America, South America, Japan, Korea, South Africa and other countries of the world; and it still appears regularly in new editions.

One encounters a person in this volume who
was completely engaged by his convictions, although
he knew that he risked his life. Dietrich Bonhoeffer
withstood the threat full of conviction. This courage
was firmly established in his upbringing, which had
the goal of fully intervening wherever one saw wrong
being done. Not without reason, his brother and the
husbands of two of his sisters were also killed by the
Nazis. Bonhoeffer's faith gave him the strength and
composure to bear the challenges and burdens.

*I believe that nothing meaningless has happened to me
and also that it is good for us when things run counter to
our desires. I see a purpose in my present existence and
only hope that I fulfill it. In light of the larger goal, all
deprivations and denied wishes are seen as negligible.*

*Bonhoeffer's cell in Tegel Prison*

During the first period of his imprisonment,
Dietrich Bonhoeffer wrote on a slip of paper:

> *Discontent – Estrangement*
>
> *Impatience*
>
> *Longing*
>
> *Boredom*
>
> *Night – deeply lonely*

And at the same time, he wrote to the parents:

> *I do want you to be quite sure that I am all right.*
>
> *… It is such a violent upheaval, that it takes a lot to*
> *adjust the mind to it. Physical wants have to take a*
> *backseat for the time being, which is something I find*
> *makes for a real enrichment of my experience. I am not so*
> *unused to solitude as some people would be, and it is quite*
> *as good as a turkish bath for the soul. The only thing that*
> *disturbs me is to think you might be worrying about me*
> *and not sleeping or eating properly.*

The family did not become discouraged, providing
each other support. After a visit from his sister
Ursula, he wrote to his parents:

> It is always so calming to find that you are so calm
> and serene through all the loathsome circumstances
> that you have had to endure because of my arrest. You,
> dear mama, recently wrote that you took pride in your
> children behaving "respectably" in horrible situations.
> In reality, we learned all of that from both of you.

With the contradiction and the tension between de-
pression and internal fortitude, Dietrich Bonhoeffer
repeatedly had to explain himself during this period.
His poem "Who Am I?" is a testimony to that.

Who Am I?

*Who am I? They often tell me*
*I would step from my cell's confinement*
*calmly, cheerfully, firmly,*
*like a squire from his country house.*

*Who am I? They often tell me*
*I would talk to my warders*
*freely and friendly and clearly,*
*as though it were mine to command.*

*Who am I? They also tell me*
*I would bear the days of misfortune*
*equably, smilingly, proudly,*
*like one accustomed to win.*

*Am I then really all that which other men tell of?*
*Or am I only what I know of myself,*
*restless and longing and sick, like a bird in a cage,*
*struggling for breath, as though hands were compressing*
*my throat, yearning for colors, for flowers,*
 *for the voices of birds,*

*thirsting for words of kindness, for neighborliness,*
*trembling with anger at despotisms and petty humiliation,*
*tossing in expectation of great events,*
*powerlessly trembling for friends at an infinite distance,*
*weary and empty at praying, at thinking, at making,*
*faint, and ready to say farewell to it all?*

*Who am I? This or the other?*
*Am I one person today, and tomorrow another?*
*Am I both at once? A hypocrite before others,*
*and before myself a contemptibly woebegone weakling?*
*Or is something within me still like a beaten army,*
*fleeing in disorder from victory already achieved?*

*Who am I? They mock me, these lonely questions of mine.*
*Whoever I am, thou knowest, O God, I am thine.*

Bonhoeffer also had to face the problem of homesickness very concretely in prison, both his own and also that of most of his fellow prisoners. And he reflected on this subject when writing to Eberhard Bethge, who was a soldier in Italy and separated from his family; Bonhoeffer wrote him about it on March 19, 1944:

> You … must be feeling very homesick during these dangerous days, and every letter will only make it worse. But surely, it is the mark of a grown-up man, as compared with a callow youth, that he finds his center of gravity wherever he happens to be at the moment, and however much he longs for the object of his desire, it cannot prevent him from staying at his post and doing his duty? …

*Eberhard Bethge as a soldier in St. Polo d' Enza, Italy*

*Clinging too much to our desires easily prevents us from being what we ought to be and can be. Desires repeatedly mastered for the sake of present duty make us, conversely, all the richer. ... We can have a full life even when we haven't got everything we want.*

Bonhoeffer with captured officers from the Italian Air Force in the Tegel Prison yard (early summer 1944); L to R: Mario Gilli, Gaetano Latmiral, Dietrich Bonhoeffer, Dante Curcio, Edmondo Tognelli, Sergeant-Major Napp, who had the photo taken.

Among the guards, Bonhoeffer had diverse friends, and because of this he also received occasional privileges. He was aware of many things outside the prison, in part through fellow prisoners who had informative visits or were able to communicate with relatives by code. In addition, he may have been able to hear English radio broadcasts. So in the early summer of 1944 he was quite hopeful because he knew that the attempt on Hitler's life would soon take place. One can conclude this from his letters. So he writes, for example, about his brother Klaus, who was active in the resistance, on the July 16, 1944:

*I am glad that Klaus is getting on so well! For a long time he was so depressed. But I'm sure all his worries will soon be over. I very much hope so for his own sake, as well as for the whole family's.*

And a week before, he also wrote to Eberhard Bethge:

> *Who knows, perhaps it (the correspondence) will no*
> *longer be necessary, we shall see each other sooner*
> *than we suspect.*

It was all the worse for him then when he received
the news on July 20, 1944, that the coup went awry.
Bonhoeffer certainly knew then that his chances of
survival were diminishing. Nevertheless, he wrote to
Bethge on July 21 that he would think "gratefully
and contentedly about the past and the present."
But the disaster continued to unfold. In the resistence,
people close to him were executed, including his
uncle, Paul von Hase, a lieutenant general and the
city commander of Berlin, whose visits to Dietrich
in prison had been a great relief for him.

*Paul von Hase (on the right) was sentenced to death on August 8, 1944, and on the same day he was executed in Plötzensee. His family, discharged from prison and fearing arrest, was taken into the Schleichers' home.*

With Knobloch, a friendly guard, Dietrich planned to escape. For the escape, the Schleicher family provided a pair of coveralls, in which Knobloch wanted to smuggle him out of the prison.

But it never happened because Klaus Bonhoeffer
and Rüdiger Schleicher were arrested, shortly before
Dietrich was transferred to the terrible main Gestapo
prison in Prinz-Albrecht-Strasse. This is where Hans
von Dohnanyi had also been held for a while, before
he was sent to the Sachsenhausen concentration
camp. Finally, Bethge was also arrested six months
before the end of the war in Italy and was brought
to the prison at Lehrterstrasse 3, where Rüdiger
Schleicher and Klaus Bonhoeffer were also held.

*Klaus Bonhoeffer*          *Rüdiger Schleicher*

On February 2, 1945, Klaus Bonhoeffer and Rüdiger
Schleicher were sentenced to death. Bethge reported
about that day:

> *When my father-in-law [Rüdiger Schleicher] looked at me*
> *and I felt quite helpless about events, he gave me a friendly*
> *nod of the head and laughed so heartily that I became quite*
> *confused. Klaus greeted me by giving a barely perceptible*
> *shrug of the shoulders, as if to show me that that was the*
> *way they had to behave now.*

On April 23, Klaus Bonhoeffer and Rüdiger Schleicher
were shot by the Gestapo.
So that he would not be well enough for interrogation,
Hans von Dohnanyi had requested a dysentery-culture
from his wife (after he had already had a bout of
diptheria and had been quite sick) because he knew
that a further illness would be less dangerous for him
than an interrogation.

But it did not save him. He was executed on
April 9 at Sachsenhausen concentration camp.
Since Dietrich was confined in the Gestapo
headquarters on Prinz-Albrecht-Strasse, the
family received few messages about him. Every
now and then they would leave him clean clothes.
Only three letters got out from this jail, the last
on January 17, 1945.

*Gestapo building on Prinz-Albrecht-Strasse in Berlin. The cellar prison
is concealed behind this facade.*

The New Year's poem "Powers of Good," which would become quite famous, arrived with one of these letters. Under the weight of the enormous burden of his family's situation, Bonhoeffer wanted to reassure them and show them that he was not despondent, but ready and able to accept whatever would happen through faith.

*With every power for good to stay and guide me,*
*comforted and inspired beyond all fear,*
*I'll live these days with you in thought beside me,*
*and pass, with you, into the coming year.*

*The old year still torments our hearts, unhastening;*
*the long days of our sorrow still endure;*
*Father, grant to the souls thou hast been chastening*
*what thou has promised, the healing and the cure.*

*Should it be ours to drain the cup of grieving*
*even to the dregs of pain, at thy command,*
*we will not falter, thankfully receiving*
*all that is given by thy loving hand.*

But should it be thy will once more to release us
to life's enjoyment and its good sunshine,
that which we've learned from sorrow shall increase us,
and all our life be dedicated as thine.

Today, let candles shed their radiant greeting;
lo, on our darkness are not the light
leading us, haply, to our longed-for meeting? –
Thou canst illumine even our darkest night.

When now the silence deepens for our hearkening,
grant we may hear the children's voices raise
from all the unseen world around us darkening
their universal paean, in thy praise.

While all the powers of good aid and attend us,
boldly we'll face the future, come what may.
At even and at morn God will befriend us,
and oh, most surely on each newborn day!

On February 28 his parents once again attempted to
reach Dietrich with a letter to Prinz-Albrecht-Strasse.
But already on February 7 he had been transferred,
through Buchenwald and other stops along the way,
to Flossenbürg.

The family heard nothing. Maria von Wedemeyer
looked for her fiancée in various camps, including
Flossenbürg, but in vain.

In the light of dawn on April 9, 1945, Dietrich
Bonhoeffer was hanged in the Flossenbürg
concentration camp. The family first learned
about it in July. As they did so often, his parents
had turned on the BBC radio broadcast. The
broadcast was a memorial for Dietrich Bonhoeffer.
Dietrich's old friends, Bishop George Bell of
Chichester and Franz Hildebrandt, both spoke.
With that, the last glimmer of hope that Dietrich
Bonhoeffer might still return was buried.

*Flossenbürg concentration camp. Execution site.*

While the death of the four men was a shocking
loss for the family, they knew that their resistance
activities had been necessary and that there had been
no other way for them. So in the summer of 1945,
Bonhoeffer's father wrote to a colleague who had
emigrated:

> I understand that you have heard that we have
> had a bad time and lost two sons at the hands of
> the Gestapo. You can imagine that that has not
> been without its effects on us old folk. For years
> we had the tension caused by anxiety for those
> arrested and for those not yet arrested but in danger.
> But since we were all agreed on the need to act,
> and my sons were also fully aware of what they
> had to expect if the plot miscarried and had
> resolved if necessary to lay down their lives,
> we are sad but also proud of their attitude,
> which has been consistent.

# A Brief Chronology of Bonhoeffer´s Life

| | |
|---|---|
| February 4, 1906 | born in Breslau |
| 1923–27 | studied theology in Tübingen, Rome, and Berlin; completed his doctorate and habilitation (1930) |
| 1930–31 | study year at Union Theological Seminary, New York |
| 1931 | instructor and chaplain in Berlin; began ecumenical work |
| 1933 | began the work of church opposition; pastor in London |
| 1935 | led the illegal preacher's seminary in Finkenwalde |
| 1937 | the police closed the preacher's seminary, but it continued illegally |
| 1939 | trip to New York in the summer; returned to Berlin for the beginning of the war |
| 1940 | employment as a "V-man" for the resistance; began working on his book *Ethics* |
| 1941–42 | conspiratorial trips to Switzerland, Norway, Sweden, and Italy |
| 1943 | engagement to Maria von Wedemeyer in January |
| April 5, 1943 | arrest and imprisonment in Berlin-Tegel Prison; lively correspondence with Eberhard Bethge, the basis for his volume *Letters and Papers from Prison* |
| October 8, 1944 | transfer to the main Gestapo prison in Prinz-Albrecht-Strasse, Berlin |
| February 7, 1945 | transfer to Buchenwald concentration camp |
| April 5, 1945 | sentenced to death by Adolf Hitler |
| April 8, 1945 | transferred to Flossenbürg concentration camp |
| April 9, 1945 | execution |

# Acknowledgments

The translator and publisher wish to thank Mr. Jerry Delgehausen for his help with the translation.

Many of the quotations from letters and Bonhoeffer's works have been quoted from previously translated volumes – with occasional minor modifications.

Bethge, Eberhard. Dietrich Bonhoeffer: *A Biography.* Rev. ed. Edited by Victoria Barnett. Translated by Eric Mosbacher et al. Minneapolis: Fortress Press, 2000.

Bethge, Eberhard, Renate Bethge, and Christian Gremmels. *Dietrich Bonhoeffer: A Life in Pictures.* Translated by John Bowden. Philadelphia: Fortress Press, 1986.

Bonhoeffer, Dietrich. *Letters and Papers from Prison.* Edited by Eberhard Bethge. Translated by Reginald H. Fuller. New York: Macmillan, 1953.

—. *Life Together. Prayerbook of the Bible.* Edited by Geffrey B. Kelly. Translated by Daniel W. Bloesch and James H. Burtness. Dietrich Bonhoeffer Works 5. Minneapolis: Fortress Press, 1996.

—. *No Rusty Swords: Letters, Lectures and Notes 1928–1936.* Edited by Edwin H. Robertson. Translated by Edwin H. Robertson and John Bowden. New York: Harper & Row, 1965.

## DATE DUE

| | | | |
|---|---|---|---|
| | | | |
| | | | |
| | | | |
| | | | |
| | | | |
| | | | |
| | | | |
| | | | |
| | | | |
| | | | |
| | | | |
| | | | |
| | | | |

# Lutheran
# Church
### 2815 N.W. 57TH STREET
### ROCHESTER, MINNESOTA 55901
### TELEPHONE (507) 285-0092